AF316837

Published by Cypress Hills Press Brooklyn, New York

Book design: Richard Tackett
http://www.richtackett.com

CORONET BLUE: THE SERIES

BY
SCOTT PALMER

INTRODUCTION

This is a reference book on the 1967 TV series *Coronet Blue,* which ran for 13 episodes. The book includes the episodes in date order, complete cast listings, numerous photos, directorial credits, and a story synopsis for each episode.

Michael Alden is an amnesiac, who must discover his real identity before the operatives of a mysterious group locate him and kill him. The key to his past might be "Coronet Blue," a meaningless phrase he remembers for some reason.

Alden was aboard a passenger ship docked in New York, lured to a secluded spot on deck, where he is told by a woman and two men that they know what he is up to-and that he has betrayed them.

They drug him, steal his identification, and throw him in the river. Sometime later, he manages to pull himself ashore, and the only words he speaks are "Coronet Blue."

He has no idea of his name, and there are no clues to his identity, as there is no record of anyone with his fingerprints. Suffering from amnesia, he decides on the name "Michael Alden," a combination of the name of his doctor and the name of the hospital where he was taken to recover.

Against medical advice, he checks out of the hospital and attempts to unravel the mystery by checking out any business or enterprise that is named "Blue Coronet," "Blue Crown," or any other similar name.

He soon finds out that he has been targeted for assassination by the same mysterious group of killers that dumped him into the river. Alden attempts to discover his own identity and that of his assailants, who are referred to in one episode as "Greybeards."

Along the way, he discovers that he speaks fluent Spanish and French, but has no idea how or why he learned these languages. He also discovers that he can play the piano and has some martial arts skill.

During his travels Alden is befriended by restaurant owner Max Spier, for whom he sometimes works washing dishes. Alden also meets and makes a friend of Brother Anthony, a monk.

The series ended before the solution to the mystery of Michael Alden's identity was revealed. However, series creator Larry Cohn said "The actual secret is that he (Alden) was not really an American at all. He was a Russian who had been trained to appear like an American and was sent to the U.S. as a spy.

He belonged to a spy unit called 'Coronet Blue.' He decided to defect, so the Russians tried to kill him before he could give away the identities of the other Soviet agents. And nobody could really identify him because he didn't exist as an American."

TABLE OF CONTENTS:

A TIME TO BE BORN EPISODE 1

DIRECTED BY Paul Bogart
ORIGINAL AIR DATE: 5/29/67

CAST

Frank Converse...........Michael Alden
Susan Hampshire...............Alix Frame
Chester Morris.....Dr. Michael Wilson
Donald Woods...................Paul Frame
Joe Silver...........................Max Spier
Louise Troy....................................Joyce
Jon Cypher..............Ewan McBurney
Bernice Massi........................Margaret
Robert Burr.............................Vincent
Marco St. John.............................Ted
James Noble.........Lieutenant Stevens
Jered Barclay....Ambulance Attendant
Jose Duval.......................Mr. Bardem
Peg Murray................................Gwen
Edward McNally...............Policeman
Robert F. Lyons............................Carl
Jane Holzer......................Party Guest

Frank Converse

Susan Hampshire

Chester Morris

Donald Woods

Joe Silver

Louise Troy

Jon Cypher

Bernice Massi

  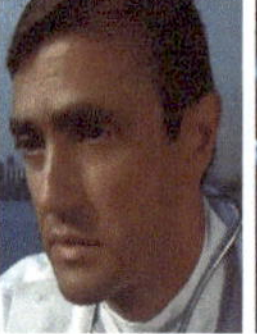  

Robert Burr    Marco St. John   James Noble   Jered Barclay   Jose Duval   Edward McNally

Robert F. Lyons

A young man is beaten and thrown from a liner into New York Harbor by two men. They remove all identification from him before tossing him overboard.

Frank Converse, Susan Hampshire

The man later manages to climb onto the dock. There, police and an ambulance are waiting. The man is disoriented; all he can do is mumble the words "Coronet Blue."

The man is put under the care of Dr. Wilson; he has total amnesia. The police have taken his fingerprints, but there is no match. The man wants to get out of there.

Uh-oh! Mike is thrown overboard!

Against the wishes of the doctor, he leaves the hospital. He decides to adopt the name Michael Alden; the doctor's first name is Michael, and the name of the hospital is the Alden Hospital.

Donald Woods, Susan Hampshire

James Noble, Chester Morris, Frank Converse

Frank Converse, Donald Woods

Alden, as he is now known, heads to a restaurant; he earns some money by sweeping up. Owner Max Spier says he can always come back if he needs work or a meal.

Meanwhile, he attempts to unravel the mystery by checking out any business or enterprise that is named "Blue Coronet," "Blue Crown," or any other similar name.

Frank Converse, Joe Silver

Susan Hampshire, Frank Converse

Frank Converse as Michael Alden

Michael meets the lovely Alix Frame at a party, then meets her father, a ship designer. It's at Mr. Frame's business that Alden discovers he speaks fluent Spanish-he also speaks French, though he can't remember how he learned those languages.

On a picnic with Alix, marriage is discussed; however one of the men who tried to kill Michael appears, and shoots at him with a rifle. Unfortunately, Alix takes the fatal bullet.

Donald Woods, Frank Converse, Jose Duval

Joe Silver, Frank Converse

THE ASSASSINS EPISODE 2

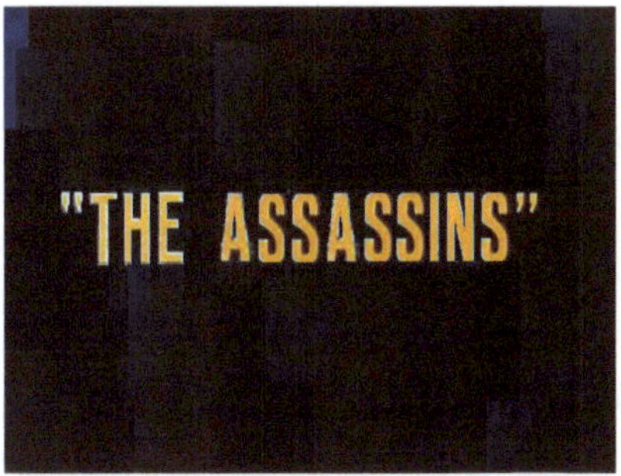

DIRECTED BY Lamont Johnson
ORIGINAL AIR DATE: 6/12/67

CAST

Frank Converse...........Michael Alden
Signe Hasso..................Lucille Sailer
Edward Binns....................Lyle Sailer
Janet Margolin............................Riva
John Vernon.......................Ali Mufti
Cal Bellini..............................Omeran
Fred J. Scollay........................Gunther

Frank Converse

Signe Hasso

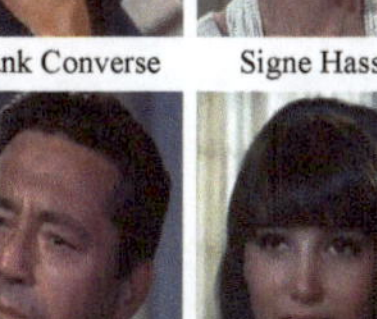
Edward Binns

Janet Margolin

John Vernon

Cal Bellini

Fred J. Scollay

Policeman

John Pleshette

Model

Mike learns through a classified ad that his parents are looking for him; he goes to meet them and his fiancee. They warmly take him back, but something is not quite right about them, and soon he realizes he's being set up.

John Vernon takes aim

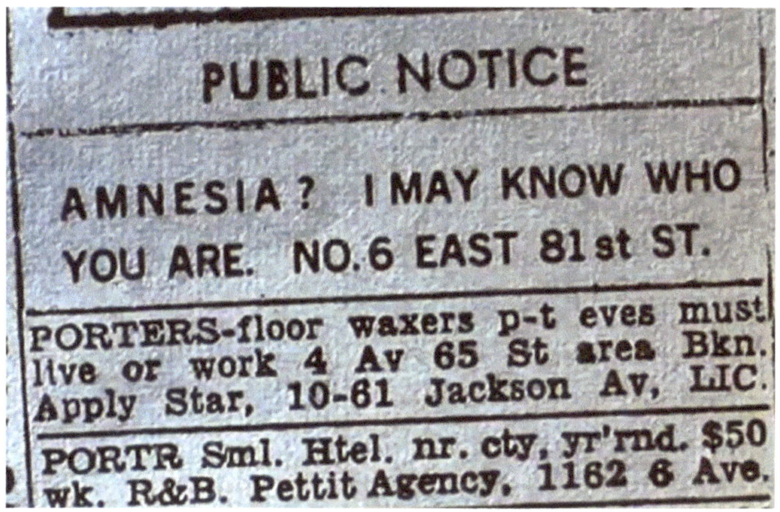

Newspaper notice

Alden questioned by the F.B.I.

The newspaper ad leads Michael to 6 East 81st Street. There, he finds a framed picture of himself in a desk drawer. A woman then appears, calling him Jerry. She says she is his mother.

After a few minutes of discussion-during which Alden says
he has amnesia-a man appears, saying he is Lyle Sailer, Mi-
chaels' father. He says that "Jerry" had been a university
student at Oxford.

Frank Converse, Janet Margolin

Edward Binns, Frank Converse

Edward Binns, Signe Hasso, Frank Converse

They came to the city they are in now, but Jerry was sup-posed to have decided to quit school when he met and be-came engaged to a girl named Riva. Riva soon shows up.

Naturally, Alden can't remember her. At a party, he is intro-
duced to Ali Mufti, an Eastern dignitary of sorts, who claims
also to know him. When Sailer slips him a drugged drink,
Alden turns violent and is taken away.

Frank Converse, Signe Hasso

Janet Margolin, Frank Converse, John Vernon,
Signe Hasso, Edward Binns

Signe Hasso & Edward Binns

After attacking a Middle-Eastern Prince, the F.B.I. questions
him, and he later discovers that he is to be the fall guy in an
assassination plot. At a soccer match, Mike is able to foil the
assassination.

He is able to dispose of Sailer as well as Mufti, who was also in on the plot. When Mrs. Sailer asks Michael how he found out, he tells her that the golf clubs they gave him were left-handed.

Edward Binns, Frank Converse

THE REBELS EPISODE 3

DIRECTED BY Sam Wanamaker
ORIGINAL AIR DATE: 6/19/67

CAST

Frank Converse...........Michael Alden
Richard Kiley..Dr. Stephen Courtland
David Carradine...........Walter Arnold
Jon Voight....................Peter Wicklow
Candice Bergen...................Enid Toler
Addison Powell..President John Marshall
Ray Middleton..............Chief Loomis
Arthur Clark....................Newscaster
Anita Sheer..................Mara Kingsley
Trent Gough.................Peter's Buddy

Frank Converse   Richard Kiley

David Carradine   Jon Voight

Candice Bergen   Addison Powell

Ray Middleton   Arthur Clark   Anita Sheer

At a New York College, Alden is the focus of experiments to overcome amnesia, but he must share a dorm room with students and earn his keep by working shifts at campus security, but this puts him in conflict with protesting students.

Frank Converse & Candice Bergen

Jon Voight, David Carradine

Frank Converse, Candice Bergen, David Carridne

Dr. Courtland puts Michael to sleep; he remembers a ship, a pretty girl, and a man with a gun. Other than that, his memories of the past are just a blur.

Courtland has to go through some red tape to continue his experiment with Alden. They have found an off campus rooming house where he can live. He is also given the job of a campus security officer.

Frank Converse, Addison Powell, Richard Kiley

Student demonstration

Frank Converse

Peter Wicklow is a rabble-rouser; he is trying to get his friend and fellow student Walter Arnold to join the protesters, but Walter says he is a pacifist-as well as a coward.

When Wicklow's girlfriend, nurse Enid Toler, tells him about the experiments with Michael, Wicklow decides to tell the school newspaper-even though what's going on with Alden is hush-hush.

The newspaper story is squashed-mostly for the protection of Michael-but this only adds fuel to Wicklow's fire; he tries to organize a large protest.

Ray Middleton

Frank Converse & Richard Kiley

Richard Kiley, David Carradine

When a sit-in happens in the administration building Chief Loomis cracks Wicklow's head with a club; Michael diffuses the situation before it gets worse.

President Marshall agrees to a meeting with the students the next day; most of the faculty signs a petition circulated by Dr. Courtland to give the students more of a voice as to the curriculum and goings on at the campus. Alden moves on.

Frank Converse, Richard Kiley

Addison Powell, Ray Middleton

A DOZEN DEMONS EPISODE 4

DIRECTED BY David Greene
ORIGINAL AIR DATE: 7/3/67

CAST

Frank Converse...........Michael Alden
Brian Bedford......................Anthony
John Beal..................Maurice Straigh
Donald Moffat...................The Rector
Joe Silver..........................Max Spier
House Jameson......................Manitee
Lynda Day....................Jenny Straigh
Berett Arcaya...........................Eileen
Joseph Mascolo.................Bodyguard

Frank Converse

Brian Bedford

John Beal

Donald Moffat

Joe Silver

House Jameson

Lynda Day

Berett Arcaya

Joseph Mascolo

Monk

After being shot, Alden finds himself at a monastery, where a monk befriends him. Noticing a stained glass window of St. Anthony resembles him closely, they set out to find the artist who did it.

Assassin taking aim

Brian Bedford, Frank Converse

Frank Converse, Donald Moffat

In broad daylight, while watching a children's pick-up base-ball game, Michael is shot by a man with a silenced gun hiding in some bushes. He is found by brother Anthony, a monk, and taken to a nearby monastery.

Luckily, it is only a shoulder wound. Brother Anthony tells
Alden that some men came to the monastery gates asking
about him, and are still hovering outside.

John Beal, Frank Converse

Brian Bedford, Lynda Day

Statue in the monastery

Michael meets the Rector, who tells him he should go to the police. It's only a suggestion, and he will not be forced to do so. For the time being, he is offered the sanctuary of the monastery.

St. Anthony, on the stained glass window-which looks re-
markably like Michael, was done by Maurice Straigh-who
also did another monastery sculpture known as Coronet
Blue. Alden must find Straigh.

With Brother Anthony's help, Michael is able to locate
Straigh, who says that he saw Michael with a girl in the park,
and modeled his stained glass window of St. Anthony after
him.

Someone prepares to shoot

Frank Converse, Brian Bedford

Straigh tells Michael that he was with a girl. Alden remembers that her name was Eileen, and has a recollection of what she looked like. Just then, a man fires a shot at Michael, but misses. The man gets away.

Brother Anthony, who has become enamored with Straigh's pretty daughter, decides to leave the monastery. It is also time for Michael to be on his way.

Frank Converse, Brian Bedford, Joe Silver

House Jameson, Frank Converse

FACES EPISODE 5

DIRECTED BY Robert Stevens
ORIGINAL AIR DATE: 7/10/67

CAST

Frank Converse...........Michael Alden
Hal Holbrook.................Cary Thomas
Mitch Ryan.....................Oscar Davis
Mart Hulswit................Carlton Hobbs
Martin Huston...........George Thomas
Michael Walker...........Robert Cooper
Joanna Roos.......................Mrs. Hope
Cec Linder...............Vincent Schuster
Phyllis Thaxter..........Eleanor Barclay
Marisa Berenson...........Mary Barclay
Lou Polan................................Deputy
Lisa James.......................Edna Farrar
Nicholas Pryor.........................Guard
John Pleshette.............................Dan
Wyley Hancock...........................Roth

Frank Converse

Hal Holbrook

Mitch Ryan

Mart Hulswit

Martin Huston

Michael Walker

Joanna Roos

Cec Linder

Phyllis Thaxter

Lou Polan

Lisa James

Nicholas Pryor

John Pleshette   Model

A mysterious photograph of a funeral reception for a murdered girl shows Alden present. Though a young man was convicted, and Alden has no memory of the event, he suspects he might be the actual killer.

Recognize this picture?

Hal Holbrook, Frank Converse

Frank Converse, Cec Linder

He tracks down Vincent Schuster thanks to the picture having been in a magazine. Schuster tells Michael that he was doing some scenes for a calendar company, and was travelling down a country road.

He saw some people gathered in a little graveyard, and snapped the picture. He tells Alden the name of the town was Jennings Grove-so Michael heads there.

He finds the picture was of a funeral. Mary Barclay, the deceased, was murdered. A young man named Hobbs hit her with a brick. Hobbs is scheduled for execution in two days.

Sign on the way out of town

Phyllis Thaxter, Frank Converse

Frank Converse, Michael Walker

Michael is asked to leave town, but he decides to stay on. He begins to ask questions about the murder, but meets with resistance from everyone he talks to.

Through the good offices of newspaper man Cary Thomas, Alden is able to finally get to see Mrs. Barclay. She does not recognize him, but gives him a book of her daughter's, which has many names.

Frank Converse and friend

Mitch Ryan, Hal Holbrook

Frank Converse, Mitch Ryan

When he says he may have killed Mary Barclay, her mother says definitely not-the man is in jail awaiting execution-he got a fair trial and was found guilty. Prosecutor Oscar Davis says the same thing.

After visiting the convicted killer in prison, Michael thinks he may be innocent, but it turns out he is in fact guilty. He is duly executed. Unfortunately, Alden is no closer to discovering his own identity.

Mitch Ryan, Phyllis Thaxter

MAN RUNNING EPISODE 6

DIRECTED BY Sam Wanamaker
ORIGINAL AIR DATE: 7/17/67

CAST

Frank Converse...........Michael Alden
Denholm Elliott..Fake Roger Crowell
Juliet Mills.............Margaret Crowell
Bramwell Fletcher.......Roger Crowell
Carlos Montalban...........Raul Estrada
Joe Silver...........................Max Spier
Ralph Purdum..........................Clerk
Alan Ansara.............................Gomez
Rene Enriquez............Carlos Sanchez
Ralph Thomas.....................Detective
Colleen Kelly.........................Waitress

Frank Converse   Denholm Elliott

Juliet Mills   Bramwell Fletcher

Carlos Montalban   Joe Silver

Ralph Purdum   Alan Ansara   Rene Enriquez   Ralph Thomas   Colleen Kelly

A marked man Roger Crowell, a refugee from a South American revolution, needs Alden's help, to hide out in his apartment and find his daughter at an American university.

Denholm Elliott, Frank Converse

Joe Silver, Frank Converse

Juliet Mills, Frank Converse

Walking down the street, Alden notices men in a car pointing a gun; he doesn't know if the target is him, or another man, who gets shot in the arm. He takes the man to his apartment and patches him up.

The man says he is Roger Crowell, who was in the Caribbean but now a certain faction is after him. Max Spier tells Michael that Crowell was running a liberal paper, then was sent to prison. Apparently he escaped and is now hiding in Michael's apartment.

Denholm Elliott with gun

Frank Converse, Juliet Mills

Joe Silver, Frank Converse

Alden heads to a university where he encounters Crowell's daughter Margaret. She is skeptical until he shows her a photograph that her father gave him.

After evading some pursuers, they return to Michael's apartment. Crowell is missing. After checking at a hotel, Alden returns home. Two men break in and start interrogating him.

Ralph Thomas, Frank Converse

Bramwell Fletcher, Frank Converse

Frank Converse, Denholm Elliott

It turns out they are not the thugs Alden suspected; Margaret says they are friends of her father, and are looking for him in order to help him. She thinks they will find her father. What no one knows however is that the apartment is now bugged.

Later, a detective shows up at Max's restaurant and asks Michael to come with him to the morgue. One of Crowell's friends has been knifed to death. Margaret is very upset about it.

When Crowell returns, it transpires he's a fake; the real Crowell is elsewhere. When he is found, the fake is arrested and Crowell is given asylum in the U.S.

Juliet Mills, Frank Converse

A CHARADE FOR MURDER EPISODE 7

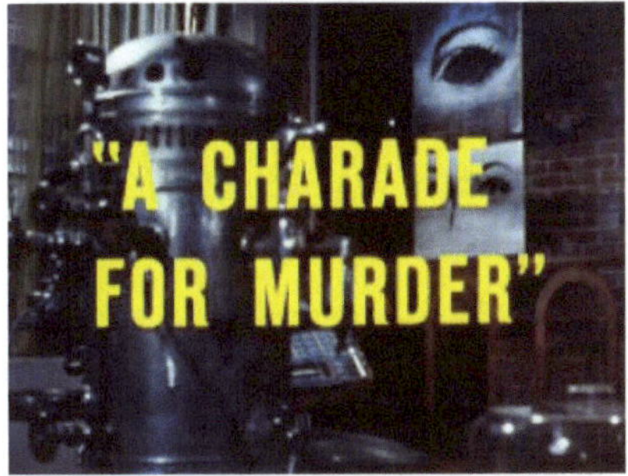

DIRECTED BY David Pressman
ORIGINAL AIR DATE: 7/24/67

CAST

Frank Converse...........Michael Alden
Jack Cassidy............................Spangler
Robert Burr.............................Vincent
Bernice Massi.......................Margaret
Brian Bedford.......................Anthony
Brenda Vaccaro...........................Julie
Joe Silver.............................Max Spier
Paul Sparer...............................Frisch
Richard McMurray.......................Vine
Richard Bright...........................Harry
Roy Scheider.......Apartment Manager
Patricia Wheel.................Edie Revere
Carol Gustafson....................Waitress

Frank Converse

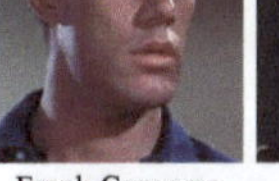

Jack Cassidy

Robert Burr

Bernice Massi

Brian Bedford

Brenda Vaccaro

Joe Silver

Paul Sparer

Richard McMurray

Richard Bright

Roy Scheider   Patricia Wheel

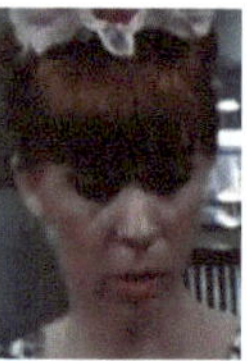

Carol Gustafson   Waitress

Anthony is lured to a strange apartment by a naval officer. Later he's accused of murdering the officer by the police when his body is found in a room where his finger prints are found.

Jack Cassidy, Brian Bedford

Robert Burr on the attack

A man calling himself Miller hires an actress named Julie to play a practical joke on Miller is in fact Vincent-one of the men who threw Alden overboard in the harbor.

Since Michael is out, Anthony intercepts a message for him, leading to a hotel, where a man mistakes Anthony for Alden, and directs him to room 512. There's a pistol on a table; Anthony makes the mistake of picking it up.

Brian Bedford, Brenda Vaccaro

Paul Sparer, Richard McMurray, Brian Bedford

Brian Bedford, Jack Cassidy

Brian Bedford, Joe Silver, Frank Converse

After a boat ride, Anthony is left in a place where Julie appears, wearing a harem costume. Meanwhile Spangler-the man pretending to be the naval officer-is shot dead with the gun Anthony had picked up.

When Anthony has had enough of the game, he returns to
the hotel; there, he finds the police, and Spanlger-dead. He
tells his convoluted story, and is soon placed under arrest.

Brian Bedford, Joe Silver

Joe Silver, Frank Converse

Joe Silver, Brian Bedford

After escaping, he heads to the restaurant, where Max and Michael help him. Max thinks he should turn himself over to the police. When they find Julie working as a waitress, they get her to tell the truth.

Vincent sees what's happening, tries to kill her, and escapes after a fight with Anthony and Michael. The police are called and Julie tells her story-which exonerates Anthony.

Robert Burr, Bernice Massi

SATURDAY EPISODE 8

DIRECTED BY David Greene
ORIGINAL AIR DATE: 7/31/67

CAST

Frank Converse...........Michael Alden
Doug Chapin...................Walter Cane
Neva Patterson..............Aunt Maggie
Joe Silver...........................Max Spier
Charles Randall....................The Man
Mark Kearney..................Benjy Cane
Miles Chapin..........................Lonny
David Hartman........................Waiter
Arthur Sussex............................Sharp
Mary Orr............................Mrs. Cane
Andrew Duncan.....Man in Straw Hat

Frank Converse

Doug Chapin

Neva Patterson

Joe Silver

Charles Randall

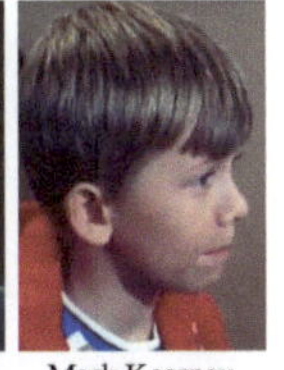

Mark Kearney

Miles Chapin

David Hartman

Arthur Sussex

Mary Orr

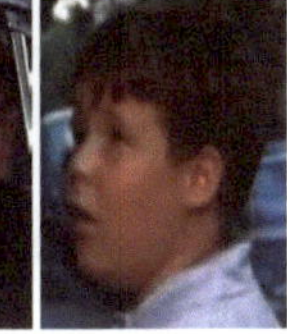

Andrew Duncan

Boy

| Man in Park | Neighbor | Woman in Park 1 | Woman in Park 2 |

Alden makes arrangements to pay a man $2,000 for his true identity, but both are pursued by ruthless hit men. A troubled boy joins him hiding out in Central Park, unable to face home responsibilities after his father dies.

Joe Silver on the phone

TV Advertisement

A man calls the Searching Eye restaurant and asks for Michael Alden. When Max asks who wants to speak to him, the man hangs up. He then calls back; this time Alden answers.

The unidentified man tells Michael that he knows who he is, who is trying to kill him, and why. The man sets up a meeting, telling Michael to bring two thousand dollars. Max gives Michael the money.

Frank Converse, Charles Randall

Frank Converse, David Hartman, Doug Chapin

Frank Converse, Doug Chapin

When he meets the man, several armed men are following; the man tells Alden to meet him at four o'clock at The Ginger Man; both run away and are able to elude those following them.

Meanwhile, young Walter Cane is told that his father has died; he is so upset, he runs away. He soon meets Michael, and they form a friendship of sorts. Michael has to meet the mysterious man, but can't shake Walter.

Michael plays the guitar

Frank Converse, Doug Chapin

Joe Silver, Frank Converse

He finally gets rid of Walter and meets the man. Unfortunately, two thugs also appear. When Alden fights them, the man grabs the money and runs. He is hit by a car and killed in the street.

When Michael runs into Walter again, he tells the boy that life is hard. Walter's Aunt and little brother are looking for him, and Michael convinces Walter to go back home.

The Ginger Man, place of the meeting

Miles Chapin, Frank Converse

THE PRESENCE OF EVIL EPISODE 9

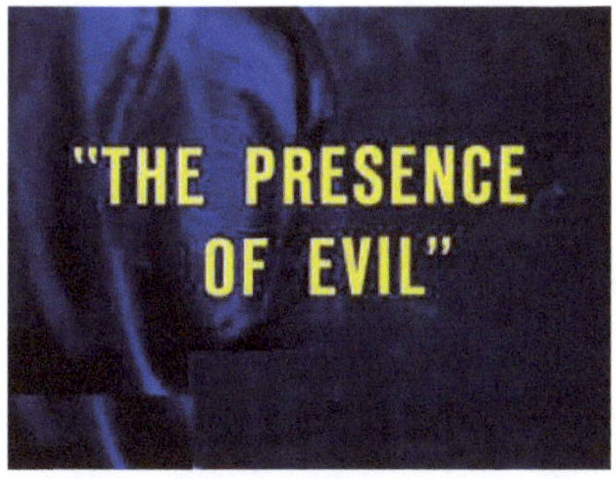

DIRECTED BY Sam Wanamaker
ORIGINAL AIR DATE: 8/7/67

CAST

Frank Converse...........Michael Alden
Brian Bedford.......................Anthony
Joseph Wiseman...........Rudi Nateseh
Viveca Lindfors.............Kyra Nateseh
Judi West.....................................Netta
Susan Tarr................................Angele
Joe Silver............................Max Spier
Carol Crist........................Folk Singer
Leonard Elliott.....................Doorman
Colleen Kelly.........................Waitress

Frank Converse

Brian Bedford

Joseph Wiseman

Viveca Lindfors

Judi West

Susan Tarr

Joe Silver

Carol Crist

Leonard Elliott

Audience Member 1

Audience Member 2

Stage Employee

A reluctant girl is used as a medium in a magic act, and a blue coronet is part of her costume. This intrigues Mike and Tony, who find the magician a strange and probably psychotic devil worshiper who won't let the girl go.

Susan Tarr, Brian Bedford

Joseph Wiseman, Susan Tarr

Brian Bedford, Joe Silver

Michael goes to see Rudi Nateseh the magician; he is told by Mrs. Nateseh that her husband is sleeping. When he asks about the blue crown, Mrs. Nateseh says it is merely a stage prop.

When Rudi discovers that Alden was asking about the crown, he tells Angele not to discuss things about the performances with anyone. Rudi says that his work is very important.

Judi West, Brian Bedford

Joe Silver, Viveca Lindfors, Frank Converse

Stage act in the theater

Mrs. Nateseh tells Michael his life is in danger. Back at the restaurant, Tony has two tickets to the show. Max is busy and can't go, so Tony takes a girl Netta. When they leave, Michael comes in with Mrs. Nateseh.

During the performance, Tony is in the audience; Mr. Nateseh has Angele in a trance. He asks who Tony is, and she
names him. When he asks about his friend with no name,
Angele says he is "Death," then has a fit and collapses.

Michael outside the theater

Susan Tarr, Joseph Wiseman

Frank Converse, Brian Bedford-looks lie Brian had
Imperial Margerine!

When Anthony goes backstage, he tells the magician it is
very important to identify his friend. Nateseh tells Tony to
bring the friend to him. So Mike and Tony head to the the-
atre.

There, they find the magician, who performs some of his tricks, then plays a cat and mouse game with them. When it's over, his wife says that he was once a great magician, but is now a sick man. Unfortunately, Michael is unable to learn anything new.

Joseph Wiseman, Frank Converse

SIX MONTHS TO MARS EPISODE 10

DIRECTED BY David Greene
ORIGINAL AIR DATE: 8/14/67

CAST

Frank Converse...........Michael Alden
Patrick O'Neal.....Dr. Andrew Perkins
Alan Alda.......................Clay Breznia
Walter Moulder.....................Dr. Ross
Dennis Patrick.......................Jackson
Joe Silver...........................Max Spier
Kenneth Harvey.....................Monitor
Barbara Blake...........................Susan
Betty Low.....................Piano Teacher
Jack Gaynor, Ed Wagner, Billy Dee
Williams............................Technicians

Frank Converse   Patrick O'Neal

Alan Alda   Walter Moulder

Dennis Patrick   Joe Silver

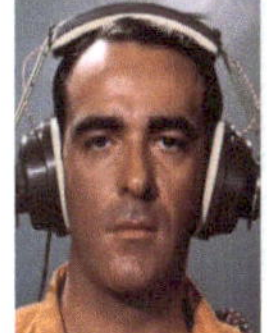

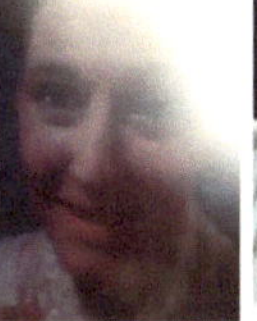

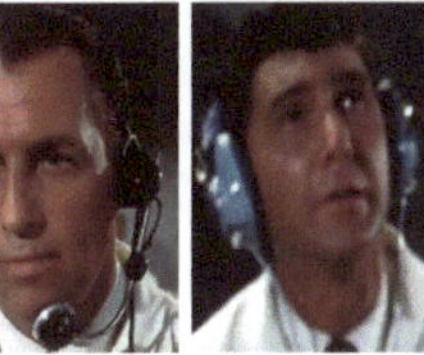

Kenneth Harvey Barbara Blake Betty Low Jack Gaynor Ed Wagner Billy Dee Williams

Patrick O'Neal listening in

Ed Wagner, Billy Dee Williams, Jack Gaynor

Frank Converse, Alan Alda

Before this happens, Michael is taking a piano lesson; he knows how to play. The pretty teacher says it's his fingers that have done the remembering.

Some men come looking for him; at first, he tries to run away, then punches the men. One of them pulls a gun, so he surrenders. He doesn't believe they are policemen-until they show their identification.

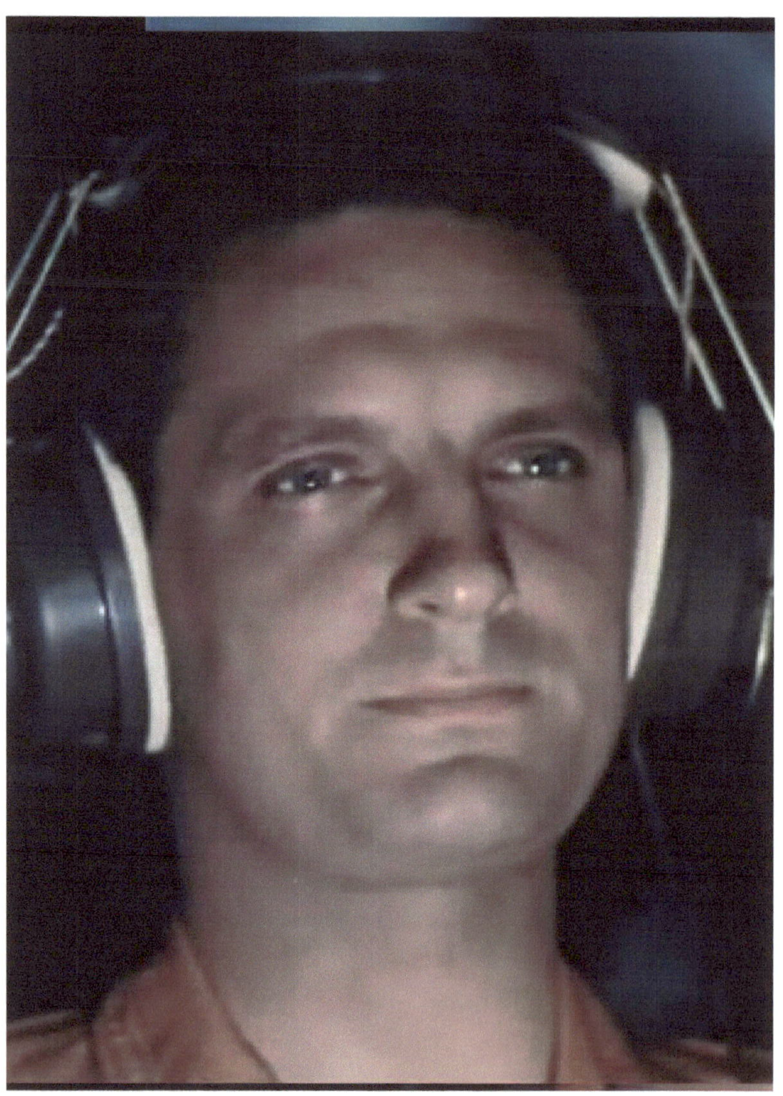

Alan Alda

Barbara Blake, Joe Silver

Alan Alda, Frank Converse

Dr. Andrew Perkins heads a space research institute; he tells Michael he would be a perfect study subject for a simulated trip to outer space. Alden refuses at first, but later agrees to take part.

Another test subject, Clay Breznia, is more than willing to take part in the experiment. Dr. Ross tells Perkins that it will be dangerous, but they go ahead with it.

Walter Moulder, Ed Wagner. Patrick O'Neal

Walter Moulder, Patrick O'Neal

Barbara Blakc, Frank Converse

Michael is shown police i.d.

After they have been in the little capsule for what would be
the equivalent of two moths, Mike and Breznia notice a rise
in the temperatures as well as other phenomenon. Is it a
malfunction, or are they being deliberately subjected to these
things?

Both start to hallucinate; Michael remembers being taught the piano as a boy. When it appears they are about to crack, Dr. Perkins has them removed from the capsule.

Michael says how he survived the "torture chamber." He tells Perkins he survived not because he forgot about this earth, but because he remembered. There are people he cares about, and people who care about him.

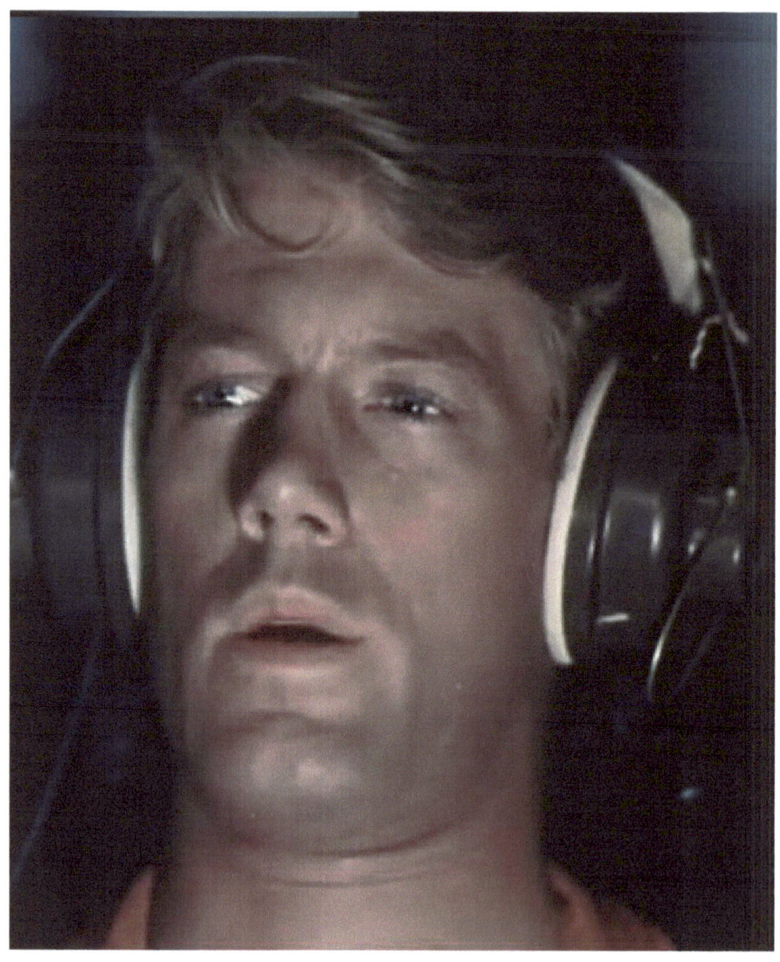

Frank Converse

THE FLIP SIDE OF TIMMY DEVON EPISODE 11

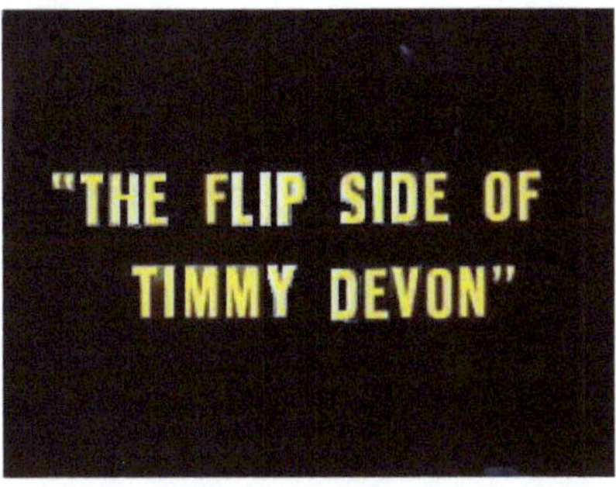

DIRECTED BY David Greene
ORIGINAL AIR DATE: 9/4/67

CAST

Frank Converse...........Michael Alden
Brian Bedford.......................Anthony
Dick Clark.............Victor Brunswick
Sally Kellerman..............Polly Walter
Peter Duchin................................Pete
Bruce Scott.................Timmy Devon
Joe Silver..........................Max Spier
Murray Kaufman..................Big Hart
Pamela Toll...............................Paula
Gene Bua, Jesse Young.............Thugs

Frank Converse

Brian Bedford

Dick Clark

Sally Kellerman

Peter Duchin

Bruce Scott

Joe Silver

Murray Kaufman

Pamela Toll

Gene Bua

Jesse Young

Girl 1

Girl 2

Girl in Pool

Alden hears a pop tune on the radio, supposedly from a dead singer, yet never released until that moment-but he somehow knows the lyrics already, and surmises that he had to have been present at the recording session. Tony joins him as they pressure the dead star's producer for information.

Maurice Kaufman, Frank Converse

Dick Clark, Maurice Kaufman

Brian Bedford, Joe Silver

First, Mike heads to the radio station that was playing the song-supposedly for the first time. Disc Jockey Big Hart swears that the late Timmy Donovan wrote his own lyrics, and the song Forget me Not definitely was never played anywhere before.

Next, he meets Victor Brunswick, head of the record company. He knows all about Timmy Donovan. He agrees to meet Alden later that night. As soon as Mike leaves, Brunswick checks out of his hotel and makes a plane reservation.

Frank Converse, Joe Silver, Sally Kellerman

Sally Kellerman, Brian Bedford

Brian Bedford, Joe Silver

Anthony then gets on the case; he is able to find Donovan's one-time manager, Polly Walter. She says she kept Timmy organized. A romance starts between Polly and Tony.

She tells Anthony that Timmy recorded the song Forget me Not in San Francisco. He then took off on his motorcycle for Los Angeles. He never made it; he went over a cliff and was killed.

Peter Duchin trio

Frank Converse, Brian Bedford

When he asks more questions and tries to see Brunswick, Anthony is set upon and beaten by two thugs, who warn him to forget about Timmy Donovan and stop nosing around.

Polly is outraged with Victor when she finds the thugs beat up Tony on his instructions. Max is even more upset; he says if he finds who did this, he will personally break their bones for them.

Brian Bedford, Frank Converse

Joe Silver, Peter Duchin

Finally, Tony and Mike discover that Timmy Devon is alive and well, and hiding in Polly's apartment. The whole thing was done to create the Timmy Devon phenomenon. That puts the kibosh on Tony's romance-as well as Michael getting any closer to discovering his identity.

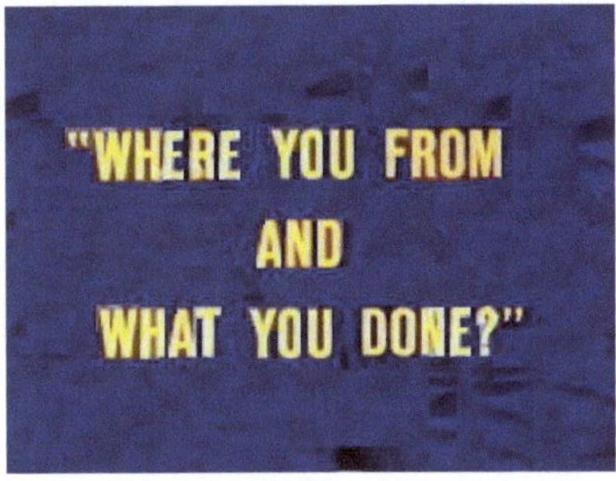

DIRECTED BY Sam Wanamaker
ORIGINAL AIR DATE: 9/11/67

CAST

Frank Converse...........Michael Alden
Laura Devon...........Ava Lou Springer
Vincent Gardenia.......The Man (Goff)
Tanya Everett.................................Sis
Joe Silver...........................Max Spier
Cliff Carpenter................Ticket Clerk
Martha Greenhouse...Philadelphia Woman
Joe Bennett..............................Stanley
Haila Stoddard...............Mrs. Winters
Frank Downing...Gas Station Attendant
Mark Gordon.......................Detective

Frank Converse

Laura Devon

Vincent Gardenia

Tanya Everett

Joe Silver

Cliff Carpenter

Martha Greenhouse

Joe Bennett

Haila Stoddard

Frank Downing

Mark Gordon

Billy

Bus Passenger 1

Bus Passenger 2

Waitress

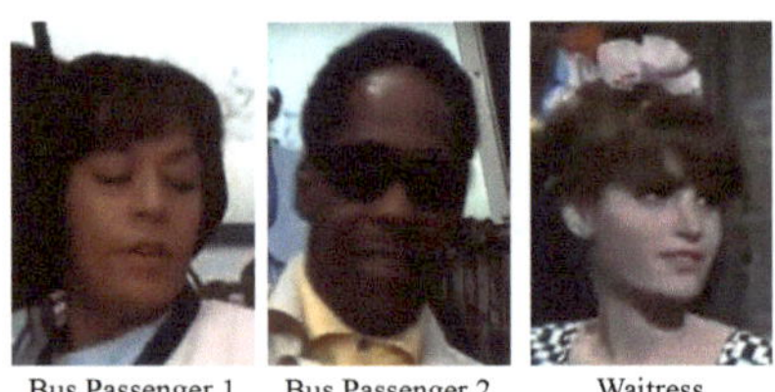

In North Carolina, Alden is befriended by a cheery, ditzy blonde aspiring folk singer. Her imaginative fabrications gradually become strange and sinister, and he's forced to find out who she is.

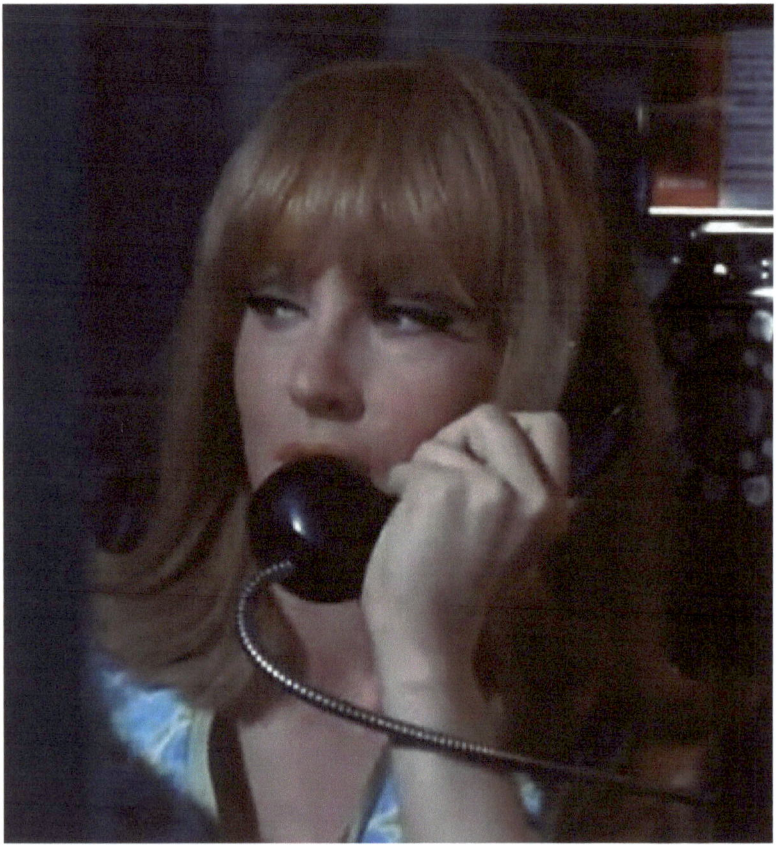

Laua Devon on the phone

Mike buys a bus ticket

Joe Silver, Frank Converse

Michael meets a woman at a bus depot; she says she is Ava Lou Springer. At first, she pretends to know him, but this is just part of her strange behavior. Mike is heading to Coronet, Virginia.

A mysterious, sunglasses-wearing man watches them get on a bus. As they head off, Ava exhibits bizarre behaviour; she bursts into song for no reason, and talks a lot of meaningless gibberish.

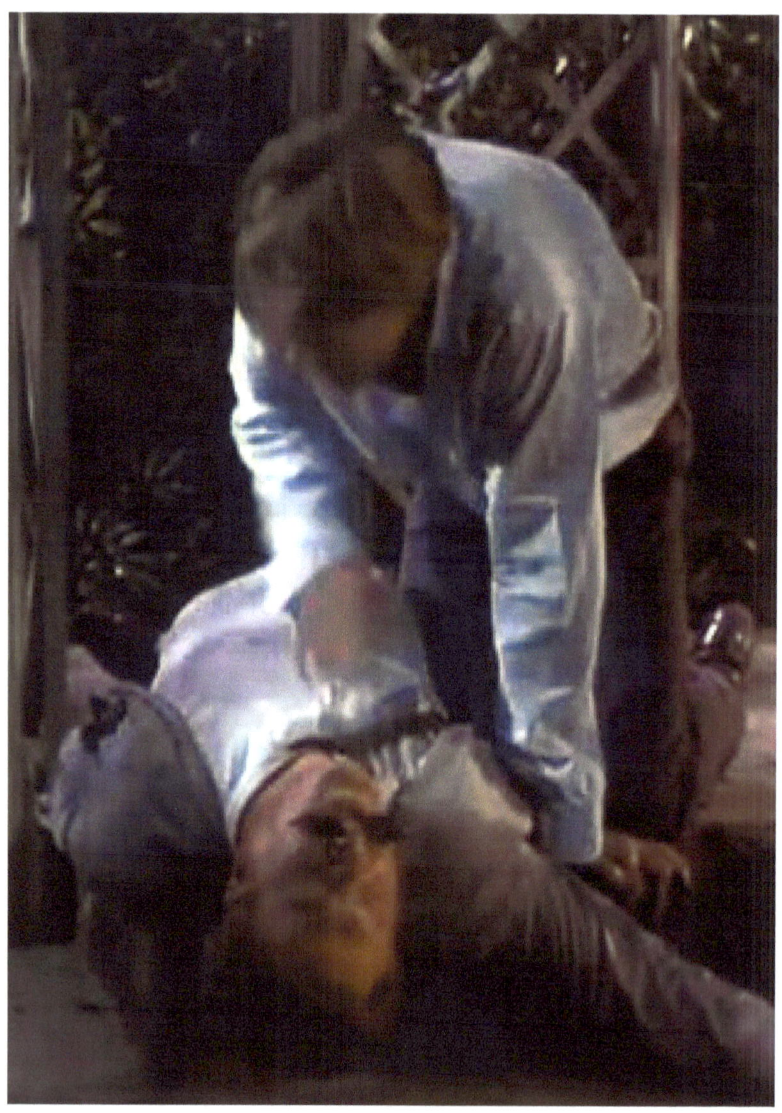

Frank Converse, Vincent Gardenia

Haila Stoddard, Frank Converse

The bus stops and Ava and Alden check into a small hotel-separate rooms of course. Ava goes to a phone booth and makes a call to New York to Mrs. Winters. She is not available.

The mysterious man-who is armed-attacks Michael. After knocking him out, Alden checks out. He takes Ava with him. Mike calls Max, who wires him money to get back to New York. Ava comes with him.

Mike decides to look up Mrs. Winters-the woman Ava tried to call several times, claiming she was her agent. When he finds her, she tells a different story.

It seems Ava-real name Avril-is her daughter. She had a breakdown after her father died, and now has a number of mental problems. The mysterious man was a detective named Goff who Mrs. Winters hired to find her daughter.

Picture found in the glove box

Frank Converse, Laura Devon

Laura Devon, Frank Converse

It seems that Avril is considered dangerous-her mother put her in a low-security institution where she caused an "acci-dent," where someone was hurt.

This time, she went too far. When she came across the unconscious Goff, she bludgeoned him to death with a log. Police come and arrest her. She now seems to be completely insane.

Joe Bennett performing

Joe Silver, Frank Converse

TOMOYO EPISODE 13

DIRECTED BY David Greene
ORIGINAL AIR DATE: 9/18/67

CAST

Frank Converse...........Michael Alden
Keye Luke.....................Yasito Omaki
Cely Carrillo..............Tomoyo Omaki
Dan Travanty............................Raffie
Joe Silver...........................Max Spier
Frank Cavestani........................Artie
Brooks Rogers....................Doorman
Sab Shimono.........................Student

Frank Converse

Keye Luke

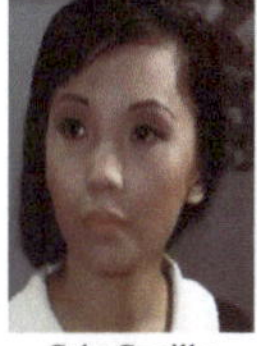

Cely Carrillo

Dan Travanty

Joe Silver

Frank Cavestani

Brooks Rogers

Sab Shimono

Fighter 1

Fighter 3

Fighter 4

Hood

Karate Man

While having some coffee with Max, Michael spies an Asian girl whom he believes he met with in his forgotten past. He calls to her, but she runs away.

Cely Carrillo as Tomoyo

Michael stacking sugar cubes

He follows her to a large building, where a number of men are performing martial arts. They see him, and surround him. When they are about to grab him, he knocks out two of them using karate. But there are too many of them, and he is subdued.

When he comes to, he is still determined to find the girl. He pays a call to a martial arts club, and talks to Yasito Omaki. Mike says he wants to sign up to take instruction.

When Omaki asks his daughter Tomoyo for an application form, Alden recognizes her as the girl he has been looking for. Omaki makes Mike promise to use what he learns only in self-defense.

Keye Luke, Cely Carrillo, Frank Converse

Keye Luke and associate

TV Poster

Mike aks Tomoyo if she recognizes him, but the girl is evasive. But she does have a drink with him. Mike's attentions to the girl seem to rub Raffie, one of the karate instructors, the wrong way. Tomoyo says he is more or less her bodyguard.

Omaki invites Mike home for lunch; he feels he would like to know him better. Omaki says Mike has great tension not knowing much about himself. He suggests that Alden work closely with Raffie.

So in the club, Raffie and Mike engage in a fight; the result is that Alden winds up with a broken arm. He is still confused, and after going to the hospital, returns to the club. The doorman says it has been closed for years.

Dan Travanty, Frank Converse

Frank Converse, Joe Silver

Hoods surround Michael

But Mike knows better; he goes inside and confronts Raffie and his gang; it turns out they are enforcers for the Mafia-that is the secret. Luckily Omaki comes along and is able to deal with Raffie.

He says he misjudged Raffie-he thought he was a good person. Mike says that the whole experience helped him discover that the place to find yourself is not in other people-it is in yourself.

Dan Travanty, Frank Cavestani

Keye Luke, Cely Carrillo